OUR DAILY PILL

VOL 2

POWERFUL LIFE-CHANGING STATEMENTS, WISDOM NUGGETS, THOUGHT PROVOKING WISDOM PILLS FOR YOUR EVERYDAY WALK IN LIFE

BY
ENOCH FLETCHER NARH

This book is dedicated to

Bishop Derek Rimson

Of Kingdom Dominion Cathedral- USA

PREFACE

Just as we all need some sort of pill when we are not feeling well in any part of our body, in the same way, I was inspired to write this simple, yet impactful book. This book is to help you as a daily prescription pill. To help you become better in life, heal some wounds, and encourage those who are down in life. To have the exact pill of encouragement, to be bold, firm, and to rise and become what God has ordained us all to become. Our Daily Pill (ODP) has so much wisdom and revelations, to help you become better than your yesterday.

These wisdom nuggets and thought-provoking statements have been beneficial to many people, friends, and folks on my social networks such as Facebook, Instagram, Twitter, WhatsApp, YouTube and among others.

This book is by popular requests from over ten thousand friends on social media who've been inspired by the words and videos. On this day, you will have it as a hard copy to enhance your daily lives. Growing as a child, I went through a lot of verbal abuse from friends, teachers and family. It often discouraged me, and I always doubted my great qualities and talents. Yet, I never gave up. They said I was not the best and could never be the best, but I kept pursuing persistently and today, I am where I am. They said I was one of the worst students ever and I had no future. There were times that they will bring out though words for me to spell and they were ready to laugh at me because they knew I would misspell. Before, I used to say the sky is the limit, but as I grew and become stronger as a leader, I understood that the SKY IS NOT THE LIMIT. If the sky was the limit, then it means there is a limit. I have come to know that you are the only one that can limit yourself from reaching far in life. Nothing can limit you, not even what they say or think about you. Today, I am the author of over five books and still counting.

May this book open you up for major transition and be the second series that will cure every kind of worry, depression, verbal abuse, low self-esteem and every uncertainty of your future. Believe in every statement you read here and pray for the wisdom and understanding to apply it in your everyday life.

Take this pill each and every day, and let it become your daily pill in all endeavors of life.

I pray that you become what you were born to be on this earth positively. Please be careful to believe, accept, and apply these pills prescribed for you to move further in life.

Get ready for more series and volumes of Our Daily Pill with The Levite. I thank God for the second volume of Our Daily Pill.

ACKNOWLEDGMENT

I would like to express my sincere gratitude to theses great ones as follows; my lovely daughter Zamora Fletcher Narh, also to you my prophet and friend Prophet Atsu Manasseh, General Overseer of Watered Gardens Ministry (Ghana) and Mama Alexina Atsu Manasseh, to my best parents Rev. Stephen Narh and Mrs. Dora Narh for all of their spiritual and material investment into my life and ministry.

A big thanks goes to my siblings Andy Cole Narh, Phoebe Agyiri Newman and Becky Narh, Auntie Vivian Childs (North Carolina) for all their support to my ministry.

I would also like to express my gratitude to all my sons and daughters of KLIC-Pennsylvania family; Thanks to lady Patrice Gregory with her enormous support to the Daily Pill series and my ministry. To Min. Deborah Fianu who's been a great asset and supporter to this project and many more, Mr. & Mrs. Joseph and Linda Larosa,

Evelyn Harriet Walwolie, Kimberly Bay, Ranmie Wilson, Ps. Randell Kau (Australia) and to all whose name time and space wouldn't permit me to acknowledge,

GOD BLESS YOU ALL FOR YOUR SUPPORT TO MY ASSIGNMENT!

TABLE OF CONTENTS

Preface..I

Acknowledgement......................................II

Contents...II

You Are God's Gift to The World.........1

You Become Your Thoughts 2

Don't Be A Pretender 3

The Power of Words 4

God Will Deliver You 5

It's All in Your Thinking 6

My Past Has No Bearing on My Future 7

Others Will Go; Others Will Stay.......8

It's for A Reason..9

They Will Ask, No Matter What 10

Not All Stories Are True 11

No Need for Many Friends 12

Learn from Your Mistakes 13

WISDOM TO HANDLE ISSUES	14
DON'T WASTE YOUR GIFT	15
GREATNESS IN THE MAKING	17
CORRECT YOUR MISTAKES FIRST	18
PEOPLE ARE QUICK TO FIND FAULTS	19
FROM STRUGGLES TO SUCCESS	20
BORN TO WIN	21
KEEP WATERING YOUR SEEDS	22
SIGNS OF A TRUE FRIEND	23
MAKE USE OF YOUR NOW	24
DECIDE TO BE FREE	25
TAKE TIME TO GROW	26
CREATE A PATH FOR TOMORROW	27
DEALING WITH YOUR GIANTS	28
I AM STILL VALUABLE	29
FROM PAIN, TO PROMISE, TO PAY	30
I AM NOT USELESS	31
EXPRESSING YOURSELF MUST BE DONE RIGHT	32

- Purpose Behind My Pain 33
- Life Without Limits 34
- Leave A Mark 35
- Make Things Happen for Yourself 36
- Have A Positive Mindset 37
- Follow the Truth 38
- God Never Fails 39
- It Will Always Pay Back 40
- Connect with The Right Spirit 41
- Stay Faithful 42
- It's All About How You See Yourself 43
- Stop Wasting Time 44
- Make Good Use of Your Time 45
- Everybody Isn't Needed on Your Journey 46
- Don't Give Up 47
- Your Set Time to Manifest 48
- Your Past Doesn't Matter 49
- Take A Positive Step 50

Be Mindful of Fake Smiles Around You . 51

Trust Is Important 52

Take the Time to Trust 53

Forgotten but Just for A Season 54

Keep Pressing On 55

Look Up to What Lies Ahead 56

My Kindness Will Pay Off 57

Be Opened to A New Beginning 58

It's Never Too Late 59

Don't Stop Climbing Your Ladder 60

You Can Do Better 61

Grace to Take Your Place 62

How Are You Using Your Tool? 63

Make the Necessary Turns 64

Attacks Leads to Higher Altitudes ... 65

Keep Your Hope Alive 66

Men Can Fail You 67

Persistent in Purpose 68

See Right 69

Blessings in The Midst of Pain 70
Our Achievements Are for The World .. 71
Don't Take People for Granted 72
Don't Judge by The Past 73
Choose Your Words Wisely 74
Power to Create Your World 75
Make A Positive Impact 76
Find Your Place 77
Don't Allow Yourself to Be Hurt 78
Don't Respond to Insults 79
Mistakes Are A Necessary Part of Success 80
Someone Else Will Honor You 81
Pick Yourself Up Again 82
Your Distractors Are in A Lower Place 83
Don't Stay in Your Fall 84
Don't Give Up on Yourself 85
You Cannot Be Stopped 86
I Am A Solution 87

- Discover Your Best Talents 88
- Don't Fall for Distorted Stories 89
- Don't Hinder Others from Being Free ... 90
- Invest Your Time Wisely 92
- What Can You See? 93
- Invest in Your Mind 94
- Are You Prepared? 95
- Don't Muddy the Waters 96
- There's Hope 97
- This Is Not Your Destination 98
- Don't Manage the Devil 99
- Only God Knows You 100
- Refuse to Fail 101

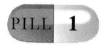

YOU ARE GOD'S GIFT TO THE WORLD

Always remember, you are one in a million and God made you so special and different from everyone in the world. You are a gift from God.

YOU BECOME YOUR THOUGHTS

Your life moves in the direction of your thoughts. You are not different from what is in your mind. Ensure to always entertain the right thoughts.

DON'T BE A PRETENDER

Pretending will make you regret not being able to show your true colors. No need to pretend. Just be yourself.

THE POWER OF WORDS

Your WORLD is FRAMED by your WORDS.
WORDS are the BRICKS by which your LIFE
is BUILT. Be careful what you say.

GOD WILL DELIVER YOU

Many of us have left the voice of God and are living in what the world says about us. How can our enemies say something good about us? Listen, they will never stand for you or say good stuff about you. They will lie on you and say all kinds of stuff about you. Don't allowing them to. When Pharaoh spoke, every charge against Joseph was dropped. They put a rape case and charge on Joseph but when the Lord spoke every charge was dropped. God can speak to the Judge or law makers to close any case or charge against you. Get ready for your deliverance.

IT'S ALL IN YOUR THINKING

Your progress is right in your thinking. Your thoughts become your movement. Your movement becomes your progress. All you need is to change your ways of thinking and everything will totally change in your life.

MY PAST HAS NO BEARING ON MY FUTURE

God will never consult your past to determine your future. Always remember, your today can never define your tomorrow.

OTHERS WILL GO, OTHERS WLL STAY

Many people will come and go but the people that stay are really connected to you. That's destiny for you! Always remember this, that God will never tie your destiny to people who left your life. Especially when you carry a great assignment on this earth.

IT'S FOR A REASON

Terrible events can lead to great happenings. Everything happens for a reason. There are many great people who had a very rough start in their childhood, but today, they have great families and are a pride to the world. I have experienced seasons in my life where things were really tough, but yet still, I never gave up. One thing I kept in mind was that the season was going to be over. My life is a testimony. As long as you don't give up, it will end well with you.

THEY WILL TALK NO MATTER WHAT

It's better to look good than to look bad
because in this life, no matter how you try to
look, people will still talk about
you all the same.

NOT ALL STORIES ARE TRUE

Most of time, not all stories are true stories. You have to take time to really know exactly what happened. You can hear one message from many different points of views. Not everyone carries the original message. Take time to know the truth about any message or rumor.

NO NEED FOR MANY FRIENDS

It's dangerous to have too many friends in life. It's ok to keep a few LOYAL friends. It's ok to DELETE some friends. The fewer your friends, the less troubles you face.

LEARN FROM YOUR MISTAKES

Life is about making time to mature and mastering your mistakes. Don't rush, otherwise, you will rust. Past mistakes help you master future mistakes and prevent you from making too many mistakes.

WISDOM TO HANDLE ISSUES

One lesson in life is, you don't blow an issue out, when you can handle it in a nice way. Many times, we blow a lot of issues out of proportion, until we realize that there was no need to do so. Wisdom makes you understand the situation before you react unwisely.

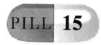

DON'T WASTE YOUR GIFT

Gifts can only be received and opened by those it was meant for. Don't waste your precious gifts on those who don't deserve it because they won't value it.

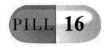

IT'S YOUR TIME FOR ELEVATION

Personal lessons in life – 3 Levels of Elevation

1. It's normal to struggle to be heard by the world in the beginning

2. When your time of elevation comes, the world will look for you

3. Learn to wait for your time

GREATNESS IN THE MAKING

The world will never make you great because you haven't gotten there yet but realize that you are greatness in the making.

PILL 18

CORRECT YOUR MISTAKES FIRST

Until the mistakes from your past relationships are learnt and corrected, you cannot be guaranteed a better one in the future. Whenever you break out of a relationship, never look at rushing into another one, because you may still have scars from your past relationship. Take time and choose to learn from your past mistakes first.

PEOPLE ARE QUICK TO FIND FAULTS

Do you know that some people are so fast to find faults with others? But it's amazing that they are unable to see what is wrong with themselves. Don't be quick to find faults, especially when you haven't taken time to correct your own faults.

FROM STRUGGLE TO SUCCESS

Struggles in life unveil God's planted success in our lives. God doesn't just allow struggles in our lives, but it's for His glory to be revealed in us. Your present struggles will yield fruits of success, if you stay persistent with God.

BORN TO WIN

You cannot and must not fail! You were born to win! Never entertain thoughts of failure, see yourself being a success! See yourself rising instead of going down. Arise from any failure in your life.

KEEP WATERING YOUR SEED

Always remember, you are a seed to the world. "Keep watering" means to keep adding to your seed until it's time to be harvested. You can only sow good seeds and reap good seeds. Decide to sow the right seeds because seeds can only bear its fruit and not any other fruits than of its own kind.

SIGNS OF A TRUE FRIEND

True friends are those who understand you for who you are and still knows you for what you're not. No one is perfect. True friends are able to handle your perfections and imperfections.

MAKE USE OF YOUR NOW

The sad truth is that many people realize that it's too late. The little things that matter are NOW. What you do now is very important. Make use of NOW very well and don't misuse it. Your future depends on your NOW.

DECIDE TO BE FREE

Your way of exit could be shown out of the bondage you find yourself in. It's up to you to decide to move or stay. See freedom from your problems and you will come out, as you see yourself free.

PILL 26

TAKE TIME TO GROW

Trees that takes time to grow bear the best fruit and have the strongest roots. Take time to grow. There's no need to rush. At times, we wish to grow faster and faster, but I've come to realize that taking time to grow makes you stronger. Your time will come!

CREATE A GOOD PATH FOR TOMORROW

Make wise decisions today! The decisions you make today will carve the path for tomorrow.

DEALING WITH YOUR GIANTS

Before you become like David, you must first learn to handle Saul and hindrances like Goliaths in the way. Everyone that must become great, will have to deal with their circumstances first.

I AM STILL VALUABLE

What we go through does not take away our value. What we go through is just temporal. Say to yourself, "I still have a great value!" Place value on yourself.

FROM PAIN, TO PROMISE, TO PAY

Behind every pain, there is a promise.
After my pain, I will have my pay.
Always remember that your pain pays
you back, with some promises and
with some great doors.

I AM NOT USELESS

People may find you useless, but you need to know that you are very useful to other people. We are more than diamonds and can't allow people (mom, siblings, love ones, family etc.) to make us feel useless.

EXPRESSING YOURSELF MUST BE DONE RIGHT

It's not bad to express your feelings towards anyone. It just has to be done right. Saying it doesn't mean that you are bad, or it wasn't really meant to be. Just be real because you never know, they could be your best friend ever.

PURPOSE BEHIND MY PAIN

There is a purpose behind every pain. A success behind your struggles and a reward behind your faithfulness. Stay in purpose and never allow the pain to hold you bound.

LIFE WITHOUT LIMITS

You were not created with limits. Lift the limitations off. They either placed it on you or you placed it on yourself. Refuse anything that limits you from moving ahead and positively achieving your greatness.

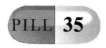

LEAVE A MARK

Don't just pass through this world. Leave a mark. Make it better than you met it. Your existence is to impact your world. Make the best impact so you can be remembered. Make a positive mark.

MAKE THINGS HAPPEN FOR YOURSELF

You have the ability to make things work for you. Don't wait for someone to make things happen for you. You have what it takes. You can build yourself positively. Things are going to turn around for you.

HAVE A POSITIVE MINDSET

Being positive has great impact on your day to day life. Being negative draws you backwards. I choose to be positive in everything I do. What about you?

FOLLOW THE TRUTH

Listen to what you know, not what you feel or what people say. Hearsay can be very misleading like your emotions. Don't judge situations by what you hear or how you feel but by what you know to be true.

GOD NEVER FAILS

You need to understand that life is very funny. Many people are not grateful when you do something for them, but there is only one person who doesn't fail. His name is God.

IT WILL ALWAYS PAY BACK

People naturally pay you back with something bad, but every good thing you do as a person, will definitely pay you back with something good.

CONNECT WITH THE RIGHT SPIRIT

The people in your life matters a lot. What is in your spirit is what controls your physical. Who you connect with in the spirit determines how things will work for you in the physical. Check connections with people around you and the people you meet. Check how you feel about them. The connections in your life can either make you or unmake YOU.

STAY FAITHFUL

Live this life by deciding to walk on the path of faithfulness. No matter what, men will definitely fail you but your faithfulness will stand to reward you someday.

IT'S ALL ABOUT HOW YOU SEE YOURSELF

How you see yourself matters a lot and not how people see you. How do you see yourself? I see myself as a king. Therefore, no one can make me feel less of myself.

PILL 44

STOP WASTING TIME

Now is the time to pursue whatever you can to change your world positively. Don't waste time because you don't have all the time to yourself. Oftentimes, we waste our time unnecessarily and at the end of the day, regrets begin to set in. If I was to waste my time, there is no way I would be sitting here writing this book.

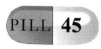

MAKE GOOD USE OF YOUR TIME

What do you achieve when you are awake? Because many of us don't do anything when we are awake. I urge you to make use of your time to achieve something better. The greatest blessing in life is to be alive and awake, but the most exceeding blessing in life, is to achieve something positive. Make proper use now that you are awake.

EVERYBODY ISNT NEEDED ON YOUR JOURNEY

You don't need everybody. There is a place in life that all you need is just that one person who believes in where you are going in life. Don't be consumed with the crowd and the people who are concerned with what you can achieve. Just a few quality friends in your life, is all you need to make your journey.

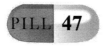

DON'T GIVE UP

There is a reward in pressing on. Never give up no matter what comes your way. Keep pressing on and moving. Very soon it will be all fine with you.

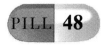

YOUR SET TIME TO MANIFEST

This is your year of manifestation. You must manifest in every way that God wants you to. As a child of God, you have no excuse other than to manifest.

YOUR PAST DOESN'T MATTER

Forget about your past and open up a new page. You cannot judge a book by its cover or current page. Your past has no bearing on your future. Refuse to dwell in the past and embrace a new page for your life today!

TAKE A POSITIVE STEP

Worries don't change situations. It's the positive steps you take that changes everything. Worrying and doing nothing about the situation wouldn't change nothing. If you need to see a change, you got to take the right step.

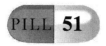

BE MINDFUL OF FAKE SMILES AROUND YOU

Not everyone who smiles at you really loves you. Appreciate the real ones around you. You will know them in your moments of mistakes and falls.

TRUST IS IMPORTANT

The better you trust, the better you think right. If you don't trust someone or have lost trust in someone, no matter what the person does, it will become very hard to think right about the person.

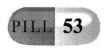

TAKE THE TIME TO TRUST

Take time to trust people otherwise they will hurt you so bad. A lot of people like you based on their own reasons that may be far from what you expect. So, you cannot put your trust in people without taking the time to know their reasons for liking you.

FORGOTTEN BUT JUST FOR A SEASON

You may feel forgotten right now, but you are not. Do everything you have to do positively, because one day it will never be forgotten.

KEEP PRESSING ON

Many people told me I was wasting my time, but I never listened to them, because I was pushing my time. Keep pressing and moving. Very soon it will be okay.

LOOK UP TO WHAT LIES AHEAD

What lies ahead of you is greater than what is holding you now. Keep looking up to what is ahead. Don't give mind to what is holding you. There is a greater glory that lies ahead.

MY KINDNESS WILL PAY OFF

I've always come to know that my kindness produces a lifetime of unforgetfulness. Keep showing kindness to people you don't know and people you do know, because one day it will bring great returns.

BE OPENED TO A NEW BEGINNING

Until you are open up for something new, you can never open a new page in your life. I urge you to step up because you have the chance to make things new this day. New day brings new strength.

IT'S NEVER TOO LATE

You are never too late in life because as long as you have breath, there is hope for a great future. Whenever you think its late, it's the exact time for you to try and start again.

DON'T STOP CLIMBING YOUR LADDER

Life is just like climbing a ladder. Don't stop climbing until you reach your destination. The higher you build your barriers the taller they become. It takes a lot of effort to climb a ladder, but if you keep climbing, you will definitely reach your desired goal.

YOU CAN DO BETTER

I am not better than you, rather, I am you. If you see me doing what I do best, it means you can do much better.

GRACE TO TAKE YOUR PLACE

God has a place, a race, grace, pace and a page for you. Keep your pace and you will have the grace to take your place.

HOW ARE YOU USING YOUR TOOL?

The same knife that can cut a bread is the same knife that kills. Use your tool positively. How your tool is used is dependent on you. But remember this, you will be held accountable for its use.

PILL 64

MAKE THE NECESSARY TURNS

You can drive straight to your destination. But at times, you have to apply breaks to make a turn to your destination. Life is not a rush. Life is taking time to make the right turns into your future. Keep your hands on the wheel and drive. The turns you make while holding the wheel to drive are important for you as you journey to your destination of greatness. Let nothing take your focus.

ATTACKS LEADS TO HIGHER ALTITUDES

When attacks come, it means you should get ready for higher altitudes. The higher the attacks, the higher the altitude you can reach. Whenever planes are faced with attacks in the air, they fly higher to avoid the attacks.

KEEP YOUR HOPE ALIVE

Hope is making time to wait until your greatness shows up. It takes people who have patience to wait to obtain God's promise. Don't give up. Keep believing in that hope because you will definitely make things happen.

MEN CAN FAIL YOU

People are prone to fail you, but there is a man who never fails. He is the God of the heavens and the earth.
He created the heavens and the earth, and he can promise you with no failure.

PERSISTENT IN PURPOSE

Passionate persistency towards your purpose, is that which yields results. Our bodies must be adjusted to the purpose of our life, and not our purpose to our body. Most of time, our body or flesh is telling us something different from what we need to do to achieve our purpose. If it's time to wake up and get things done, just do it. Don't let anything stop you.

SEE RIGHT

You need the right sight to see beyond your today. Many people have eyes but can't see beyond what they are now. See something greater than what you are, and you will thank God you did.

BLESSINGS IN THE MIDST OF PAIN

Most of the time, it's in the midst of your pain that you encounter your blessings. You can find good news in every bad news. In the midst of your pain, that's when blessings show up.

OUR ACHIEVEMENTS ARE FOR THE WORLD

It's great to achieve a lot in life, but you need to understand that when it comes to achievements, it was not just meant for you but for people coming your way and the world at large.

DON'T TAKE PEOPLE FOR GRANTED

Never look down on anybody. Many people have hidden gifts the world hasn't seen yet. One of the things you don't ever want to do in life is ever take anybody for granted.

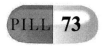

DON'T JUDGE BY THE PAST

Never use someone's past mistakes to judge his better future. What you knew someone to be in the past, might not be the same person he/she is today. God doesn't concentrate on our past, neither should you.

PILL 74

CHOOSE YOUR WORDS WISELY

If the world is going to honor and respect us, then we must be extremely careful of what we say. The same mouth that can settle a dispute, is the same one that can cause a war. You need to make the world a better place and not a bad place. We all have a role to play when it comes to our social media. Never use any platform, use the right platform. As a matter of fact, we can create good things and impact our generation positively. The next generation is going to be worst, based on how worst we are today.

POWER TO CREATE YOUR WORLD

You can create your own world based on how you want to see your world. Speak the right things no matter what. You were made with the power of creation and you can also create better things, Speak the right things and it will come into reality.

MAKE A POSITIVE IMPACT

You are not on this earth to just watch others become great. You are here to make a positive impact. You mean a lot to this world. Don't waste your time. Remember, you are here to make a statement.

FIND YOUR PLACE

Life is such that you can only be where you are celebrated and not where you are tolerated. Reside where you are celebrated and not where you are tolerated. If you waste your time in a place where you are tolerated, you can never become anything good. You can be totally rejected and uselessl. You are worth being celebrated by the very people in your world.

DON'T ALLOW YOURSELF TO BE HURT

People will hurt you no matter what.
Don't waste your emotions with their
hurts. Don't allow their hurts to hurt you
Live above hurts.

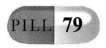

DON'T RESPOND TO INSULTS

You are no different from those who curse and insult especially when you decide to reply back to them. Never waste your time because it's very draining to waste your life and emotions trying to fight others back. No need to do that.

MISTAKES ARE A NECESSARY PART OF SUCCESS

If you are afraid to make mistakes, you will never excel. Every great man is full of mistakes. It doesn't mean you plan to make mistakes, but it's the fact that you take risk to learn faster and correct yourself, so you never make those mistakes again. That's what makes you greater. Overcome mistakes and understand that you have another chance to make things right.

SOMEONE ELSE WILL HONOR YOU

Sometimes the people around you will not honor you. Oftentimes, those you do not know will honor you the most. Always remember that a Prophet is not honored by his own people. Most of the time, it's those around you that will suffer because they were around you but never have the opportunity to receive the best inside of you. I have decided to never take people around me for granted.

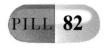

PICK YOURSELF UP AGAIN

The fact that you are down today doesn't mean you will stay down forever. Pick up something out of your fall and rise again. Arise and Shine, gather some lessons and jump out of that problem you are in.

YOUR DISTRACTORS ARE IN A LOWER PLACE

Those trying to pull you down are in a much lower place than you. Don't stoop to their level. Whenever you give them attention, they will be able to get you to be on the same level with them. Remember, there is a purpose over your life and you cannot allow them to distract you in any way. You have to achieve something better.

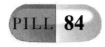

DON'T STAY IN YOUR FALL

We are still down because we have found ourselves there, but we can choose to rise up and we will see ourselves up. It is true that one can fall, but it's never true that one cannot rise. It's time to rise up from any fall in your life, right now. Don't stay in your fall.

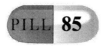

DON'T GIVE UP ON YOURSELF

Do not give up on yourself when people give up on you. People will always be people. You must see beyond what they are doing towards you. Find a way to let go of their schemes to give up on you.

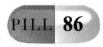

YOU CANNOT BE STOPPED

The more they try to stop you, the more you must move a little step higher. Every step we make in life, in a positive direction, is bound to change your current limitations. Whenever you are stopped, see it as an opportunity to move further in achieving that positive goal.

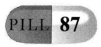

I AM A SOLUTION

Always remember you are a solution and not a pollution. You are on this earth to make a great impact and not to create war. It's very important that you understand this. Wherever you find yourself, no matter the situation you may find yourself in, understand that you can turn things around and make it better. No need to make situations worse. Instead, be a solution.

DISCOVER YOUR BEST TALENTS

When you find the best talents and gifting's in you, the best in the world will also find you. In this 21st century, your gifts are the start to your greatest blessings in life. Apart from all the qualifications in life, you need to nurture your gifts and talents because they can make a lot of difference in your life and around the world. There are a lot of positive talents and gifts that you can use to change your world.

DON'T FALL FOR DISTORTED STORIES

People will normally distort the story in so that those they want to convince, will not hear the exact truth. Most of the time, not all stories are true stories. If you don't really take the time to get the details of the story; how, when, and what exactly happened, then it's very wrong to conclude any story that you hear.

DON'T HINDER OTHERS FROM BEING FREE

The spirit of crab will never allow their very own friends to come out. They all want to be in chains. They all want to bring themselves out. My question is, if you don't want to move out and be free, why must you pull those that are trying to do something good with their lives down? I refuse every crab spirit. The world will be a better place if there was not anyone trying to prove he is more powerful than the other. Can you imagine two great people coming together to join hands to do something greater instead of being greedy? Let's come out of the crab circle, which means no one close to you or in the same circles with what you do or want to achieve, can never do it.

INVEST YOUR TIME WISELY

Matured men don't waste their time finding faults with others; they wisely invest their time into making themselves better.

WHAT CAN YOU SEE?

As far as your eyes can see, is what God will give to you. God cannot give to you what your spirit man cannot see or envision. Train your spirit to see far and beyond.

INVEST IN YOUR MIND

This modern world isn't ruled by muscle and physically stout men, its ran by thinkers. Greatness is not vested in bodily structure, but how well and far one can think. Invest in your mind and you shall one day be celebrated.

ARE YOU PREPARED?

God will never give you what you have not been prepared for. God is our Father and He is willing to give us all things, but he won't entrust a blessing into our hands that He knows we cannot handle. Everybody wants to be blessed, purposeful, good marriage, etc. But how many have actually prepared, invested, and nurtured themselves for the desired blessings? Decide today to invest into yourself for the blessing you desire. If God finds you capable, He will release it to you.

DON'T MUDDY THE WATERS

Don't muddy the water brooks that you drunk from in the past, someone else might need to drink from it. There's no need to bad mouth or speak ill of someone or something that's no longer in your life. If it was a blessing to you and it no longer is, remember it might be a blessing to someone else.

THERE'S HOPE

A living dog is better than a dead lion. The fact that you have life is proof that God isn't done with you yet. Others had the things you desire and wish for but are dead and gone. Life is more important. There's hope as long as there's life.

THIS IS NOT YOUR DESTINATION

Your condition is not your conclusion! Many times, we settle in our present conditions thinking that's what God intends for us. Understand this, whatever condition you may find yourself in today, is not your final destination. Rise and keep moving.

DON'T MANAGE THE DEVIL

You don't manage the devil, rather, you damage the devil and your enemies by damaging their schemes. Respond by saying no to managing the devil.

ONLY GOD KNOWS YOU

People don't know you that much when they start claiming they really know you. People only use a little clue from your past, to judge the best ahead of you. Nobody really knows you better than yourself and the one who created you. Just make sure you are real to your maker and not bother what people say about you or how much they think of you. Only God knows you and can make the best out of your future.

REFUSE TO FAIL

Make the decision to not be a failure. The world awaits the manifestation of your greatness. Please don't let them down.

OTHER INSPIRING AND LIFE TRANSFORMING BOOKS BY ENOCH FLETCHER NARH

i. "A Call to Praise and Worship"
ii. "The Purpose of Praise and Worship"
iii. "Why A Call to Praise and Worship?
iv. "Praise and Worship in The Church"

WATCH OUT FOR THE FOLLOWING BOOKS...

i. "Something Inside So Strong"
ii. "The Levite's Worship Manual"
iii. "There's Got to Be More"
iv. "Break Forth with Praise and Worship"
v. "Are You A Worshipper?"
vi. "Life Changing Prayers"

For copies of any of these books, please contact all notable bookstores, online stores, and the website below

www.levitefletchernarh.com

Our office in Pennsylvania;

Enoch Fletcher Narh Ministries

Pennsylvania

540 N 56th Street

Philadelphia, PA, 19131

Tel: 011 610 991 6659, 011 610 991 6103, 011 267 385 1819

Or

Contact our Ghana Office

P. O. Box CO – 834 Tema, Ghana W/A

Tel: +233 243- 789760 +233 244 296 366

Facebook: Levite Fletcher Narh, Levite Fletcher Narh II, Levite Fletcher Narh III

Made in the USA
Columbia, SC
20 February 2022